It's In The Blood:

A Trilogy of Poetry
Harvested from a Family Tree

Dedurie V. Kirk
Alice Kirk-Blackburn
Cheryl A. Kirk-Duggan, Ph.D.

River Vision
Austin, TX

It's In The Blood:
A Trilogy of Poetry
Harvested from a Family Tree

Dedurie V. Kirk
Alice Kirk-Blackburn
Cheryl A. Kirk-Duggan, Ph.D.

Library of Congress Catalog Number: 96-92292
ISBN 0-9652304-0-6

Published by:

River Vision
P. O. Box 6386
Austin, TX 78762

Dedication

To our ancestors, whose perseverance, by the grace of God, made possible this opportunity.

Acknowledgments

To God:
for blessing us,
over and over and over again.

To our family:
for supporting us.

To our friends:
for encouraging us
with their excitement about the book,
and comments to make it a better book.

To Carolyn C. Johnson:
forever a teacher/friend.

To Rosalind Oliphant:
for sharing her book industry savvy.

To Lenora Birch, Emma Sue Jordan
and Imogene Harris:
for providing information
to make this work complete.

Contents

Part 4

Part 1

Alice Kirk-Blackburn

It's in the Blood

I've been through a lot of things
And right now
I can't explain why.
Many pains, many disappointments
And many dreams
Died with a cry.

I've examined myself to see
If I'm bad or good
To determine if I'm holy
Or worshipping gods of wood.

I've looked into the storms
That are raging in my life
To see if I'm on the straight and narrow
Or just putting on a face
And acting real nice.

I've meditated long and hard
From cathedrals and country chapels
To the high church and the low
Even to the rug on my bedroom floor.

I've cried and I've cursed,
I've laughed and I've joked
But I've not been able to determine
If my life is real
Or some cruel hoax.

I've tossed and I've turned
I've asked moon and stars
Spoken with the sun and the wind
Again and again.

The only peace I've found
The hope to bridge me through the flood
Are the words my sweet Mama said,
"Oh, child, it's in the blood".

CRIES
OF THE
WILDERNESS

In the Pits

"Oh Lord God of my salvation, I have cried day and night before thee: Let my prayer come before thee: incline thine ear unto my cry; For my soul is full of troubles: and my life draweth nigh unto the grave. I am counted with them that go down into the pit: I am as a man that hath no strength: Free among the dead, like the slain that lie in the grave, whom thou rememberest no more: and they are cut off from thy hand. Thou hast laid me in the lowest pit, in darkness, in the deeps.

Psalms 88:1-6

I feel like I'm in a tomb, dear God.
I can't breathe in here.
Is this the place of the dead,
Or is there anybody down here with me?

Is this solitary confinement
Because I've done something wrong?
Or is this my protection
From a worse thing?

Am I to hide and not tell anyone I'm here?
Or am I to pretend I'm somewhere else?
It's kinda hard to pretend,
But, never-the-less. . . .

What am I to do
When my back is against the wall?
Am I to come out fighting
Or stand here and fall?
Who's in the yard keeping score anyhow?
How do we know when we win?

What do I do when the lights go out?
Do I stand here and grope in the dark?
Do I wait for someone
To come with a candle?
Or do I just pray long and hard?

It's hot in here God.
And I'm tired of waiting around.
If this tomb is for my death,
Please just let me die.
If it is not, oh God,
Please then explain why.

Make haste, O God, to deliver me;
Make haste to help me, O Lord.
...thou art my help and my deliverer;
O Lord, make no tarrying.

Psalms 78:1,5

Help

*My days are like a shadow that declineth; and I
am withered like grass.*

Pslams 162:11

I'm withdrawing more and more, oh God
Do you see what's happening to me?
If this is what you saved me for
Then you could have let me be.

Burnt out and empty:
Are not words enough to describe
The vacuum and the hurt I feel
And the pain that's deep inside?

Where do I turn?
Which way do I go from here?
I can't die and I can't go mad;
And I can't bear this another minute.
I'm caught in an astonishment
Of how things have come to be.
Please do something quick,
Reinforce my heart
And let me know you are in it.

I don't mind the circumstances
And I don't really mind the pain
I just have to know that you are here
To know that to live is gain.

Options

Have these last years been wasted?
Is bitterness my only gain?
Am I still to search on farther
Or take long walks in the rain?

Is this it?
What I've worked and waited for?
Why is there nothing within?
Is this how the old life ends?
Where does the new one begin?

What's the matter God —
You don't like me anymore?
Is it something that I've done
To cause You to shut the door?

Where is that in the Bible?
Must be something I've overlooked.
I don't remember reading such-a-thing,
Can you tell me
Which chapter and what book?

I can't speak of more,
Because it's all so incomplete.
I can't even emit a yell for help.
All I know is the torture of my soul
It's up to You, oh God,
To take the very next step.

*Will the Lord cast off forever and will he be
favorable no more? Is his mercy clean gone
forever? Doth his promise fail for evermore?
Hath God forgotten to be gracious? Hath he in
anger shut up his tender mercies? Selah*

Psalms 77:7-9

My Despair

In God have I put my trust: I will not be afraid what man can do unto me. For thou hast delivered my soul from death: wilt thou deliver my feet from falling, that I may walk before God in the light of the living?

Psalms 56:11,13

My God, you've never failed me yet.
But I feel myself
Falling more and more each step.
I feel a scream about to come forth
Then it vanishes
And again it's no more.

Help me from this.
Rescue me for I'm slipping.
Day in and day out
I feel the drain.
Now, I'm quite sure
There's nothing that remains.

How am I living?
Only by your spirit, I'm sure.
There are points of such numbness
Life within me seems quite obscure.

I wander and I move,
I 'm like a clock that's wound too tight
I can't seem to break this
Though I try with all my might.

Oh, the darkness of the night
It's all so black and bleak,
I've lost my sight.
I grope about, unable to quit
Like one wandering in the wilderness
who's lost their wit.

If I could stop now, I surely would.
I'd stop right here and die.
But there's a greater power moving me on
And just now, I can't say why.
How much longer do I have to wait?
How much more is there to bear?
Oh, I'm so very tired now,
All I feel is my despair.

The Quest

Am I murmuring, oh God?
You're the one that ought to know.
If I'm complaining, oh God,
You'd be the first to say so.

I remember way back
It seems so long ago
I was willing to settle for less
Than God's best would bestow.

I tried so hard
To take what I could see just then
But you, with a strong arm
Said, "Not so Love, stop here and start again."

You then began to unfold
My heart's greatest desire
You led me to what I longed for
And revealed your plans that would transpire.

I, with tears and carefulness,
Began to search your will.
Tell me God, speak to my heart,
Am I on the right pathway still?

How did all this come about?
I never asked for much "to-do".
I just wanted to praise your name
And keep my eyes on you.
Is this where I'm supposed to be?

Why is everything so scattered?
Why am I at my wits end
And I feel so bruised and battered?

Oh, I could scream...
I can't take anymore...
I want to quit now...
Or go through the door.

The Reply

Oh, don't give up my child,
Don't give up so quick.
I know how I've made you, my child
And I'll not let you get licked.

I'm a doctor who's never lost a patient,
I'm a father who's never lost a child.
To think that I'd just let you go
Would really be quite wild.

I' m taking you to a place
Where I can give you much more
I'm taking you, do hold on,
Please don't shut the door.

You've waited a long time
And I 've waited much longer still
Do trust me now, my child,
To bring you to my perfect will.

Alive Again

"I feel almost alive again!"
Isn't that something to say?
Almost alive again,
It's the dawning of a new day.

Almost alive again!
Hope is breaking forth as a small light
So small, barely can be seen
But it signals my life is going to be all right.

Almost alive, I'm beginning to breathe again
Oh what excitement and thrill can mean
Being brought back to life
And the joy it can bring.

Coming up from the wilderness and out
through the pit
My happiness I can't express.
I feel the spring bubbling up again
Giving me inner peace and rest.

Have you been through the wilderness
And just come up from the pit?
How do you verbalize
Without having a glory fit?

Almost alive again!
What I've hoped and prayed for
Is coming true.
Do believe me when I say
What's happened to me
Shall happen to you.

The Voice of God

How can anyone believe
I heard the voice of God today.
How can anyone believe?
"It was just the wind", they'll say.

"You? - you heard the voice of God?
How did He talk?
What did He say?
How did you know it was
The voice of God — anyway?

"When did you get
To the place that you can say,
'I heard the voice of God,
He spoke to me one day'?

"You really don't have proof
It was the voice of God.
Was it a tapping on the roof?
Was it a knocking very hard?

"Lets look at things realistically
If indeed you would.
You heard the voice of God, you say?
For your sake, I really wish you could".

On, on, on went the chatter
Harder and harder they beat the gums.
Heavier and heavier my heart did weigh,
Yet none could erase the voice of God
I heard that day.

The Wilderness

I didn't bring you out the wilderness
To let you fall again.
I didn't bring you out the wilderness
To let you die in your sin.

I didn't bring you out the wilderness
Just to show I could
I didn't bring you out the wilderness
To worship gods of wood.

I did bring you out the wilderness
To give you life brand new.
I did bring you out the wilderness
Because my love was just for you.

I did bring you out of the wilderness
Oh, how wonderful you look.

I brought you out of the wilderness
For life eternal with me
You're booked!

Stage Left

Has life ever disappointed you
And all you felt was your despair?
Have you ever felt the drain of pain
And thought that no one would ever care?
Have you ever tried with all your might
Yet you could not break the chain?
And did you ever think
That you would never live again?

Take all the disappointments
And pile them in a stack
Push them all behind you
And never take them back.
Walk away with joy in your heart
Know what this thought really means:
God has many, many blessings
Just waiting in the wings.

*"Because thou hast been my help, therefore in
the shadow of thy wings will I rejoice."
Psalms 63:7*

*"...but this one thing I do, forgetting those
things which are behind, and
reaching forth unto those things which are
before...."   Philippians 3:13*

Part 2

Dedurie V. Kirk

It's in the Blood

Athletes, musicians, writers, students
It's in the blood.
Mechanically inclined, gifted, talented, artistic.

All those Washington kids play an instrument.
It's in the blood.
Each one of the Wright children is smart.
It's in the blood.

What about the Mayo and Lawrence brothers.
Can't they play ball?
It's in the blood.

You ever hear those Kirk men sing?
It's in the blood.

Both of the Johnson sons can really preach.
It's in the blood.

Those Mosely sisters sew like its store bought.
Those Kirk women sure can write.
It's in the blood.
It's in the blood.
It's in the blood.

Blackness

I wear my blackness
Everyday
In what I do
And what I say.

Family

We gather at deaths
Send congratulations at births
Sit down to dinner on holidays
Rejoice at graduations.
Nothing has to be said with everybody around
When someone is missing,
The circle is incomplete.
We are family.

Special trips planned in the summer
Coming from east, west, north and south
To an appointed place
And an appointed time
Gathering together to stay connected
In between births and deaths
Weddings and holidays
Forging the links
Completing the chain.
Family time is communion time —
A time for celebration.

Four Letters and a Lifetime

Would you give up your life for me?
Would I give up my life for you?
That's what those four letters are all about
Anyway.
L-O-V-E, unconditionally.

God loved us and gave His Son.
His Son loved us and gave His life.
That's the definition of love,
L-O-V-E, unconditionally.

The innocence of a child,
The openness, the warmth,
The caring, the sharing.
No preconceived notions.
I offer myself.
I accept you as you are.

Emotion, commotion,
Disagreement, reconciliation.
Give, take, 50-50, 60-40, 70-30.
Whatever it takes.

We establish a firm foundation
On the principles of God's love.
We build on our hopes and dreams.
We strengthen each others weaknesses.
We construct our relationship,
This marriage on L-O-V-E
To last a lifetime.

No More Labels

I am an African American Woman.
As plain as day
Like white on rice
No doubt about it
That's all you see
That's all you know about me.

Do not call me out of my name
Do not label me to fit into a mold
You can handle.
I am not a girl.
I am a grown woman
Handling the responsibilities
Of a woman,
Like a woman.
I am not a welfare queen.
I work.
My mother worked.
My mother's mother worked.
My mother's mother's mother worked.

Do not make assumptions about me
Nor categorize.
I am not fatherless.
My father and mother
Were married for 37 years
Until the day my father died.
I did not come from an abusive home.
I had a wonderful childhood
And grew up in a loving family.

I am not unique or different.
There are many African American women
Just like me.

I am not my job title.
My life is not defined,
Nor my identity gained
By the work I perform
From 9 to 5.

My definition was solid long before
You ever laid eyes on me.
My identity comes from my God
And my family.

I'm not your hoe (whore), your bitch,
Or your dog to be slapped.
I am an African American woman;
A woman to be respected.
I am not yours to be abused
Or to be used.
My femininity
Need not take a back seat
Or a subservient timid role.

Do not tag me as nontraditional.
My choice of career was just that.
A choice.
I'm not trying to prove anything
To you or anybody else.

If you can not call me
An African American woman,
It's your loss.
Don't call me at all.

I've made my choice,
I'll follow it through.
African American women
Have done it for years.
Women of African descent
Have done it for centuries.

A Pastor's Heart

What does it take to have a pastor's heart?
How do you hold up
Under the tremendous pressure?
How do you empty your mind and your soul
from all of the burdens
That are cast on the Lord through you?

How did you know
How to help me swallow
The bitter pill of repeating the words
"Lord, let your will be done"
Even when we both knew
What the outcome would be?
How do you keep the floodgates from opening
When you've had to be strong
For so many others
Who were shedding painful tears?

What keeps your heart strong,
From being ripped in two?
Who assists you in standing
With integrity, dignity and respect?
What makes your heart open
To midnight, long distance calls
From those who are no longer in your charge?
I don't know what or how,
But I do know who.
And I thank God
For giving you a pastor's heart.

Relinquishing and Reclaiming

I relinquish,
I turn loose,
I let go of
They, them, the man . . .
Those nameless ones
Who I have given so much control
Those people, places and things
That I have made into little gods,
Whom I have given more power and authority
Than they in reality have.
Whom I have let my mind believe
Control my life.

I relinquish,
I turn loose,
I let go of
They made me,
They wouldn't let me,
I should have,
Could have,
Would have.

I reclaim,
I declare,
I pronounce,
I acknowledge
God,
The Father Almighty,

Omnipotent (all power and authority),
Omnipresent (present in all places at all times),
Omniscient (knowing all things)
One.

I reclaim,
I declare,
I pronounce,
I acknowledge
The activities that will enhance
My mind and body.
Spirituality, divine guidance, peace
Direction, purpose, dreams.

I can,
I will,
I'm able.

I reclaim,
I declare,
I pronounce,
I acknowledge
Me.

Setting Up Residence

Where does your mind reside?
In what happened yesterday
Or what could happen tomorrow.

In happy childhood memories
Or dreaded adult realities.

In someone else's definition of you
Or the evolution of your true self
As defined by you
And only you.

In newspaper declarations
About your age, race or sex
Or in the recognition of the things
That make you tick.

Does your mind dwell on weaknesses
That render you unable
To move forward in your life?
Or does it accept your existence
As one with
Good points, bad points,
Good days and bad days,
With hope for balance
And a better tomorrow?

Do you cultivate your mind
With the riches of this life
That will help it to expand and grow?
Or do you acquiesce the outside attempts
To corrupt, poison and stunt
Your development?

Does your mind
Make its habitat
Among the thoughts of things
Which went unsaid
Or words uttered
That cannot be retracted?

Is your mind's hangout decorated
With the furnishings used
In trying to take care of and sort out
Other peoples business?
Or is it draped
With the fabric which takes care of the
business at hand . . . its own.

Physical residences are chosen
With care and concern,
Taking in consideration,
Safety, beauty, access, ...

Choose where your mind resides as carefully.
If not consciously chosen,
It will be subconsciously set up
Among polluted thoughts,
Destructive ideas, and infertile memories.

Cultivate the ground,
Till the soil,
And set up your mind's residence
In fertile ground.

Sanctuary

A safe place, a hiding place.
For just a little while
Time can be still.
And with time stilled
So is my soul,
To allow me to catch up with myself.
Find my center of gravity,
My equilibrium,
My balance.

Is it real or imaginary?
Can such a place truly exist
When all parts
Of my conscious and subconscious being
Are pulling and tugging,
Questioning and wondering,
Demanding and directing
All in different directions?

Is there such a place
When my world has been turned
Upside down and inside out,
All that I used to count as routine
No longer exist?

Where is this place
When I cried and cursed,
Sought understanding and found none,

Woke up this morning
And wished I would have died
In my sleep?

What is this place of peace
In the midst of
Rain, hail, sleet, snow,
Typhoon, tornado, hurricane,
Twister of emotion, turmoil, wrought pain,
When nothing is alright
And not even a sunshiny day
Makes it better?
Where can I be safe
When I've said I will never cry in public
And find myself shedding uncontrollable tears?
What is my next turn,
When rock bottom
Seems to be a dwelling place
Right before slipping off the edge
To the bottomlessness of eternal night,
Dread and doom
Of a not merciful death
Of a living existence?

What are the directions to this place
That if I am to continue this existence
Before stepping over the ever thinning line
That separates sanity and the sheer madness
I seem destined to reach?
When I thought I knew
But discovered I didn't.

When hope, anchor, and courage
Dissolved before my eyesight
As I watched helplessly,
Unable to grab hold
And keep them from losing
The shape of their existence.
This is hell and I'm not even dead yet!

Nothing has ever prepared me for this.
Nothing could ever prepare me for this.
Going down,
Sinking
Beyond the last grasp
Of any possible redemption . . . .

Sanctuary!
Could this be it?
I've listened, been taught,
Heard of the mercy seat.
Do I dare presume to touch it
Less known sit on it?
Holy ground . . . . Lord have mercy!
Am I truly about to know for myself
Who God is?
Can I really meet Him for myself?
I've come here before many a time.
But there is new definition within the walls.
The look is different,
The presence is different.
No longer just a place, a building . . .
This is Holy Ground!

The Holiness of God is defining
Sanctuary to my soul,
To my spirit.
Speaking in an unutterable language.
I am
Because and only because He is.
He is.

Can my palate be redefined
To taste of his goodness?
Has my vision been altered?
I thought I saw
But now I know I see.
Oh thank you Jesus!
Thank you God!
Thank you Holy Ghost!

Look for and to no other source
Because of the finiteness
Of their being.
Infinity?
Mathematics
can not — will not — ever
describe infinity.
Infinity can't be boxed.
Omnipotence can't be boxed.
When broken to the fundamentals
Of my very existence,
The Creator and Sustainer of my existence
Allowed me to see with unveiled eyes,
Experience, void of preconceived notions,
Experience with the nakedness of a newborn.

It is sanctuary.
The sanctuary He gave me.
The safe place.
The hiding place.
The place where my soul can be still.
The place that if I can just get there,
I know,
That I know, that I know
It will be alright
Because I am in His presence,
His dwelling place.
Oh yes.
It is real.
No imagination or synthetically induced
Temporary fix.
Sustaining.
My sanctuary.
Can't tell you where yours is.
Mine may not be yours.
Can't tell you how you'll arrive there
Or when.

But who,
I can tell you who.
God will take you there.
He's prepared it for you.
He will restore your soul.
He will renew
all of you —
your mind, heart, spirit, soul.
You will be calmed and stilled in this place.

When searching, seek Him.
My place — WVUMC.*
Your place,
God knows.
He prepared it for you,
Before you.
Because He knew you.
And He knows you.

Looking for your sanctuary?
Look for God.
Not your definition
Or someone else's.
Not some likeness.
Not some
preconceived notion.
Look for God.

In your search
He'll guide you.
And when you find Him
He'll be at your sanctuary.

—————————

*Windsor Village United Methodist Church
Houston, Texas

I'm Waiting on the Dawn

There's a saying that
It's always darkest before the dawn.
Well, I sure hope dawn is soon
Because it's pretty dark out here.

I'm real serious when I use the word "hope".
That's about all there is to hold on to.
Friends get tired of listening
Others don't seem to understand.

Is there always a happy ending?
NO, I surely know one thing if no other.
Every ending is not a happy one.
And even endings sometimes don't end.
They keep recurring in our memories.

But to survive in this world,
Hope has to be unending.
So just to survive for this day
I'm hoping — and waiting on the dawn.

Blown Away

From nothing, to something
In no time at all.
I am just an instrument
Chosen by God.
He could
have picked anyone,
Yet He chose me.

How awesome it is
To see Him at work
With once blinded eyes
That now are open — with recognition
Of who God is
And how He works.

I caught a glimpse of God
And it blew me away.
He provides everything.
The instrument must simply be willing
To be used,
To see what fine melodies
Will come forth.

He plants the seed of an idea.
The instrument must act on the seed,
Believing it has the potential to grow
And will grow
Because of the seed's origin.

God not only gives the seed,
But He gives the increase.
All the instrument must do
Is practice that which
It already knows
And be faithful
To that practice.
God will send everything else
In time
And on time.

Need water?
God will provide rain.
Need encouragement?
God will send a voice
From an unexpected source.
Unaware of the next step?
God will open a door
That you didn't even see.

You know what you want
But don't know how to make it work?
God will send someone by your way,
Not even aware
Of your particular concern
And let them minister
To your need.

Isn't that awesome?
Isn't that God!

And then you come
To recognize His work.
That it's not you.
But it's God.
He could have chosen
Any of His creation,
But He chose you.
Hold on,
Because you are about to be
Blown away!

Part 3

Cheryl A. Kirk-Duggan

It's in the Blood

In the blood,
My blood.
Blood: courses through my veins,
The blood of my ancestors
Those magnificent folk
Who help make me, me.
In the blood
The DNA
Floats my energy
My self, my character
Myself,
Me.

In the blood
There is hope
If I love me,
And love my community well.

What else is in the blood?
In the blood
Lies life;
In the blood
Lies death.

Death from Leukemia
The white cells get too smart
And out grow the red.

In the blood lurks AIDS
A monumental killer
We keep pretending ain't there.
AIDS kills by day
And kills by night
When do we stop pretending?

All of us
The least of these
The most of them
All targets for DEATH.
Death — that's in the blood.

No longer can we pretend,
Hold our heads in the sand;
AIDS is here and will kill
If we keep pretending
And keep doing what we think
We are grown enough to do,
And we ain't.
And we ought not.
AIDS is in the blood;
AIDS kills.

In the blood
Is life.
The life of hope, resurrection.
Did Jesus have to die?
Whether he did or not,
Who knows?
Some say: "He had to die:
Remission of sin requires blood sacrifice."

Some say: "No he didn't have to die:
If we lived like Jesus lives,
Sin would be transformed
And we would all know salvation."
Either way, it's in the blood.

In the blood,
Nutrients, Life force;
Don't make no difference
The color of your hair,
Your eyes, your skin
The amount in your pocket book,
How much you weigh
Who you know
Where you been
Where you might go
Blood knows no difference.
Blood knows blood:
A; B; AB; O;
Positives, negatives, Rh factors.

Ain't it a trip?
Millions are victims
Of homicide and genocide;
Billions of dollars spent
Fighting each other
The hate,
The violence
Racism; classism, sexism,
All those other isms--

Political, social, historical masochisms
The selling of souls,
The lost of integrity,
The endless wars of ethnic cleansing;
And the blood knows no difference
Healthy blood gives life
Diseased blood, no blood produces death;
Dig it?
It's in the Blood.

To Mother

(Naomi Ruth Mosely Kirk)
On the Occasion of her 32nd Wedding Anniversary
(1979)

Nee?[1] Where are you?
What are you doing?

A mother who has given much
Sacrifice often the order of the day—
Reading a novel—
Cutting out a three-piece outfit?
Ministering at the high school,
Musing over a magazine,
Listening to classical music,
Bedded down for the night?

And tomorrow—
What will you be doing?
Above and beyond
The daily schedule of things—
Question: Who are You?
Who am I?
Who do you and I desire to be?
What makes us happy?

---

[1] Nee was my Father's endearment for my Mother.
They married February 2, 1947. My father joined the
eternal June 29, 1983; My mother transcended this life
October 29, 1989.

Realize the positives and negatives
Of self and life:
Aim to grow more.
Let that beautiful person inside
Continue to blossom,
Even as the rosebuds of your Mother's garden
Hold up their heads at dawn.

A wish of happiness is yours
A desire for hermitage—
All elements for enduring security
May not come.

And then?
What do you owe?
Have you paid your dues
Have your debits and credits balanced?
Is there a song in your heart?

A wish for continued happiness is yours.

God bless you, both.
We three children love you madly.

To Daddy

(Rudolph Valentino Kirk)
On the Occasion of his 32nd Wedding Anniversary
(1979)

A King, sitting up on your throne
You are affectionately know as:
Rudy, Doc, Rudolph, Daddy, King-fish . . . . [2]
The list is long
Of special names
Friends and loved ones dub you.

You have always been a King
The Chieftain of your many flocks:
A leader.
Leaders must toil, you know
Leaders must face defeat, but
Rise up again and bounce back.

Leaders must face difficulty but not succumb
Leaders must love,
They in turn will be loved;
Leaders must cry,
But no tears of despair;
Only tears of hope, courage, determination.
Leaders must be like a giant torch
In a great storm.

---

[2] My father was appointed Deputy Sheriff in Lake
Charles, LA, in 1951. He was the First African-
American Deputy Sheriff in the State of Louisiana since
Reconstruction.

You are a leader.
Your plight in life
Has never been destined to be easy.
Since you have been called of a chosen few
To be a leader,
Then you have no right
But to persevere, by Grace.

In your desire to continue to lead and ascertain
May God continue to bless you.
May God, the Supreme Architect of the
Universe
Grant you wisdom and endurance,
Happiness and peace of mind.

God bless you, both.
We three children love you madly.

Something Died

Something died.
Something died inside me.
And that hurt so bad —
Some power, some force,
Had rent the curtain
Of my inner temple
Of sanity, spirituality, and shalom.
The ecstasy and joy
Of a week ago
Dissolved in a raucous cry
Of tears —
As pain exorcised itself
Midst the trauma of disbelief.

Jobs, Games, and Time

I have a job.
I am not my job
My job is not me.
Sometimes I get bored.
Sometimes I ask,
What's the point?

The question is not the job
But how I feel
About the job;
About doing the job.
But having a job is not
Like being Job.
Spelled alike
Sounds differently.

A job is a challenge
To be with people
And to do well.
What happens when
Others don't do
Don't care
Don't take care of business?

My job is mine,
Not yours.
My goal is excellence.
Not perfectionism or victimization.

I have thoughts
And so do you.
The game of life
Is an exercise
In self-actualization.

My job supports me,
Supports my family.
I work hard;
I do not retard
The growth of me,
Of my company
Of you.

"This Little Light Of Mine"[3]

This Little light of mine,
I'm going to let . . . .
Let what?
Let it shine!
Really?
Whose light is this?
It's God's, not mine.

We keep talking about light
The light God gave to me
That's shaped by the impact
Of my ancestors,
And extended family
And all of those
Who've crossed my path,
Day in and day out
Morn, noon and night.

That light has flickered
In the souls of many
Not so uptight and idolatrous
As to deny God thought enough
To give them the light of day.

---

[3] Traditional African-American Spiritual

Where time drifts
From moment to moment
As hearts beat
Babes sleep
And rain goes pitter patter
And many folks think it don't matter.
But their stuff's so flaky
They pretend to be God
'Cause life's so hard;

When things get shaky
Remember the Light.

Light shines when God is here and there;
Our lives are dear
Tho' we hurt and no one's near
To dry the tears of pain and fear:
The light still shines and God is here
God cares and ne'r forsakes
Anyone, any light, any time, anywhere.

Say hello to God inside:
Let your light shine.

Birth: "Mary had a Baby" [4]
Thinking Back on Dedurie's [5] *Birth*

What an angel you are:
For days and months,
Leading up to your birth.
We waited in eager anticipation;
Our joy and curiosity about each stage
Of Mother's pregnancy.

So beautiful was the day
Advent gone and Epiphany near.
You no longer lay
In a cozy womb
But your little soul
Sprang forth, making a joyful noise.
Our excitement was not contained!

So beautiful are you!
Your eyes dance;
Your disposition, so wonderful.
You are the past and present,
Our ancestors arise from your being
We celebrate your coming.

---

[4] Traditional African-American Spiritual
[5] My younger sister.

May God give us the wisdom
To love, nurture, and teach you
The ways of noble love, truth, and joy
That you grow and soar,
Beyond the skies of blue.

Celebrating Nobody-ness:
Two Voices

Voice One:
No One, Not One

I'm Nobody.
Pay no attention to Me.
Give Me,
No respect, no love,
No attention.
I'm Nobody.

I'm Nobody.
I gave Me away.
There is no Me.
Do you see Me?
I do not see Myself,
I cannot feel Me.
I do not know
The physical Me.

Is there a difference
Between Hot and Cold?
Between where I start
And you stop?
Who am I?

You said I don't exist.
I bought your line.
I couldn't fight anymore.
I have no fight left—
No fight left for Me.

I am your punching ball,
Your stomping mat,
Your padded cell.
I gave up on Me—
I am Nothingness,
No one, not one.

I am your garbage disposal:
Dump anything and everything
On Me, in Me.

I have no rights.
I owe You all obedience,
I made You God.
You are my God.
My covenant with You
Gives You all rights,
Gives Me none,
Makes Me an extension of You.
I have no choice.

I have become scapegoat
Victim, Battered one,
Poor in Spirit, no spirit,
Absent of self, no self.

I am woman, man, child,
I am all people,
I am Not Me.
I am Nobody
I am Not Me.
What Now ?

Celebrating Nobody-ness:
Two Voices

Voice Two:
Hopeful Self, You & Me

I hear Your Pain,
Despair, Angst,
No one, Not one,
Empty.

I have stood in Your shoes,
I come to Hug you
With My Voice.
I come to let you Know
God says:
"Here's Your Choice:
I love You.
I made You in My Image.
All the Voices in Heaven
Cannot drown out the sounds
Of your pain, your whimpers,
Your Nobody-ness."

God says,
"Oh, my Child
My dear, lonely, aching Child
You need not walk alone."

"I am here in the stars,
The moon, the sun.
Feel Me, know Me.
I wash the mighty shores.
I fire up the volcanic ovens
In the earth."

"Feel my warmth,
I shimmer in the Spring,
I shout hosannas in the Fall,
As new buds peek
Through their
Garments of green,
As gentle leaves go to sleep
See Me."

"I am in You
And Others,
Let Me take your hand."

"I call You not with
Agony, ache, anguish,
Distress, disquiet, discomfort
Hate, hardship, humiliation
Scandal, shame, sadness
Insult, indignity, injury."

As God, I say:
"Life is full of rocky paths,
These difficulties come,
But I stand with You."

"Your life is an invitation
To dance, sing, grow with Me.
I give you freedom
To choose the music
That delights you."

"If the chosen music brings pain
I still love You,
I love You through Your Nobody-ness
I love You to Somebody-ness
I am Hope and Joy,
I am Life.
I am in those who know Love
And Love You.
You are Lovable,
You have Meaning,
You are me."

"I love You."

Ain't Got No Family

No family stands here for me;
No family.

No one talks to me.
No one listens.
People talk at me
People order me
People disregard me
I fare no better with my family.
No family stands here for me;
No family.

No one cares if I live or die;
No one cares that
I've been buked and scorned.
And I've been talked about;
I've been called ugly:
I live ugly
I've been teased and taunted;
My soul feels dead.
No one cares if I live or die.
No family stands here for me:
No family.

I feel so old;
So ugly, so tired.
Does it matter if I live or die?
Does it matter if I go to school?
Who cares?

Teacher calls me dumb
Says I have a problem
Says I am a problem
I hurt so bad at school
Sometimes, I just want to die.

Sometimes I'm so hungry,
I can't think straight:
I hunger for food, for a smile,
For one word, just one word,
From somebody who thinks
I worthwhile,
That I can make it.
No family stands here for me:
No family.

Where is my family?

Would having a baby make me family?

No Lickin'

No lickin':
Refers not to eating cold treats or chicken,
But means no beating.
Beating is not about love;
Beating concerns frustration and anger,
Often a sense of
What do I do
With this misbehavin' child
Who gets on my last nerve,
Who embarrasses me?

I'm grown and they're not!
I pay the bills;
What am I to do?
I'll go up 'side their head.
But when you do; its not love.
Lickin' means I'm right,
'Cause I'm bigger.
Lickin' means:
You gotta do it my way.
No lickin'.

No lickin' I say,
Of man by woman,
Or woman by man.
Of children by either;
"Spare the rod, spoil the child."
Means: No Lickin'.

"Spare the rod, spoil the child."
Means: "Pull the child close!
Like a shepherd does a lamb.

No lickin':
'With hand, or fist, or pipe, or belt;
Or words, or intimidation, or threats.

No lickin'
No abuse, no coercion, no embarrassing;
No taking for granted, no name calling
No violence
No lickin'.

No one has the right
To misuse and abuse.
The broken noses and jaws,
The broken spirits and hearts,
The injured self-esteems:
Grieves God's heart and mine, too.

Can't we do life differently?
Can't we learn to communicate,
To appreciate,
To have our feelings?
But handle them sanely and remember
It's all energy; we have a choice.
To give voice to love and not hate
Let's do before too late
No lickin'
No lickin'
No lickin'.

And It Rained

And it rained.
Millions of drops of moisture
Rushed from the atmosphere;
Pelted down creating
A dynamic symphony—
The toneless notes,
Embroidering a moment in time,
When thoughts of you emerged
And I sighed.

The music continued,
Impressions on my mind's eye
Eloquently danced
To the sounds
Against the roof top,
Against the windows,
The street

I felt;
I sighed;
I had loved;
We live to love again.

Rockin' Chairs

Rockin' chairs:
Moving, creaking in the summer time;
On Granny's porch.
As we sip iced tea and sodas,
To the faint melody
Of a mild breeze
That evokes sounds
From the sycamore tree
As flute players
Evoke sounds from their instruments.

Oh so mellow
Oh so comforting
The flute player's tune
And sitting on Granny's porch.
Musing to the sounds
Of that old creaking rockin' chair
That's put many a babe to sleep.
Did Granny make any teacakes?

Romance

Cherries, strawberries
Delectable, delightful, delicious;
A squeeze, a smell, a laugh
A kiss; hmm——, good!

The lush grass between my toes
Tickle, titillate
Like the hairs on your beard
When I lay on your chest.
Your heart pulsing, beating
A rhythm of joy unseeming!
Oh, what ecstasy
As a chorus of birds chirp;
And the ocean roars.
The music of our dreams,
When first we reach
The mountain top.
Higher than Mt. Rainier,
Surpassing Mt. Everest.

Oh, joy!
Sweet rapturous joy!
Beyond compare;
I sob a tear of release.

Could heaven be so good?
Bring one so high?
So far
Beyond the outer galaxy
In a moment of passion
Of sweet romance
With you?

I count
The moments, the hours, the seconds
When we again scale summits
Of communion:
God, you, and me—
As candles flicker in the distance
And lightening bugs do the same:
Whether autumn or spring time
At dusk, at dawn:

We'll be there together.
An anthem
So melodious, so tender,
So sublime, so juicy.
Ambrosia could not be as sweet,
As the remembrances
Of the last time
I saw your face
And you saw mine.

Sisters

I thought of her today,
All silky and brown,
Lying in my arms
Such hope, such possibility,
So tiny, so new,
I loved her.

I loved her while in her mother's womb;
I loved her first-born newness;
I love her today.

My sister,
My pal;
My great friend,
My buddy, my confidant.

I sing soprano
To her alto;
We enjoy each other's company;
And we know we are different.
And we know we are alike:
The same bloodlines
Course through our veins.

My sister
Is a No-Nonsense Woman.
She is awesome and cool;

She cares about
Old folks, young folks,
And those in between.

She takes seriously the question:
"Am I my brother's or my sister's keeper?"
She'll read you and say yes:
Within reason.

She'll give you her last.
And if you blow that?
She won't bad mouth you:
She'll just be through with you.

She is her own woman;
In obedience first and foremost to God;
She is a great spirit,
And a marvelously infectious laugh.

We've cried together, mourned together,
Worked together, played together,
Prayed together, worshipped together,
Loved each other well.

Miles separate us:
But there's no distance between
Our hearts, our spirits, our being:
After all, we're sisters.

Part 4

Our Family Tree

The Kirk Family History

The Kirk Family Reunion Chronicle

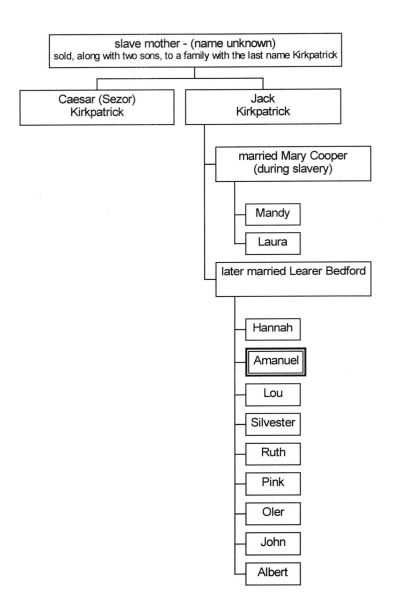

slave mother - (name unknown)
sold, along with two sons, to a family with the last name Kirkpatrick

Caesar (Sezor) Kirkpatrick

Jack Kirkpatrick

married Mary Cooper (during slavery)

Mandy

Laura

later married Learer Bedford

Hannah

Amanuel

Lou

Silvester

Ruth

Pink

Oler

John

Albert

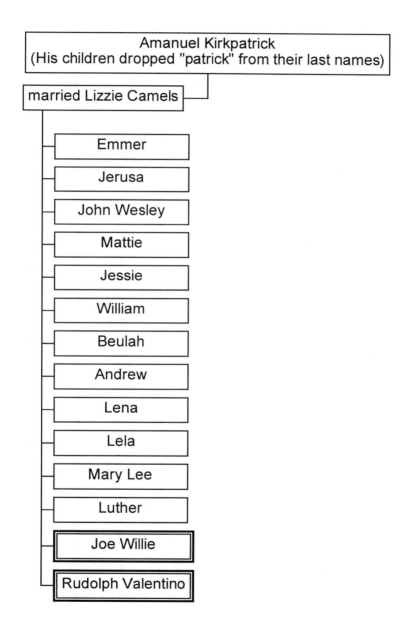

Amanuel Kirkpatrick
(His children dropped "patrick" from their last names)

married Lizzie Camels

- Emmer
- Jerusa
- John Wesley
- Mattie
- Jessie
- William
- Beulah
- Andrew
- Lena
- Lela
- Mary Lee
- Luther
- Joe Willie
- Rudolph Valentino

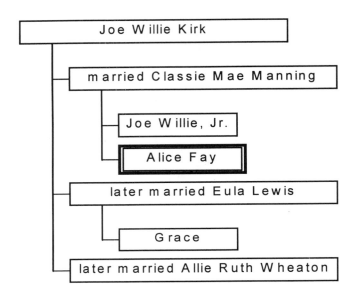

Joe Willie Kirk

married Classie Mae Manning

Joe Willie, Jr.

Alice Fay

later married Eula Lewis

Grace

later married Allie Ruth Wheaton

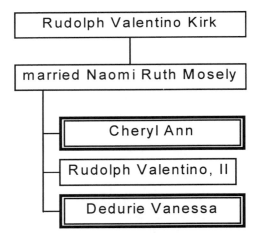

Rudolph Valentino Kirk

married Naomi Ruth Mosely

Cheryl Ann

Rudolph Valentino, II

Dedurie Vanessa

History of the Kirk Family
by
Lenora Birch

The first hints of the past generations of ancestors was passed on to me from my grandparents, Monroe and Mary Kirk, during summer vacations with them as a child.

My quest to find out officially where they came from began when it was known that the Kirk Family Reunion would be held in Louisiana (July 14 - 16, 1989), where I found records of Great Grandfather, Caesar Kirkpatrick's marriage license.

A co-worker, who was also seeking his family roots, suggested that I check the Genealogy Department of the Shreve Memorial Library in Shreveport, Louisiana. After searching all day on my second trip there, I found form "1880 Louisiana Soundex" K520 - L144, which was the Census Index which listed where they came from. The census record shows they came from the state of Tennessee.

It was passed on to my grandfather that they went by the last name of Birch. Their mother was sold to the Kirkpatrick family and she was brought to Claiborne Parish, along with her two small children, Jack and Caesar. Here, they took the name Kirkpatrick during slavery.

Caesar married Laura Veals on July 10, 1867. They had seven children: Mollie, Monroe, Henry, Andy, Will, Joseph (Joe), and Jimmy (Jim).

Jack married Mary Cooper during slavery. Their children were Mandy and Laura. Later he married Learer Bedford. Their family consisted of nine children: Hannah, Amanuel, Lou, Silvester, Ruth, Pink, Oler, John and Albert.

They lived in Mt. Obie, Cherokee and Bethel communities near Haynesville. They were farmers and many of them are buried in the Meadors Cemetery.

It should be noted, we are all Kirkpatricks. The records show Kirkpatrick but the reason some are Kirks is because our foreparents stopped writing the "patrick".

From the Kirk family, many have excelled in various walks of life: ministers, policemen, city councilmen, teachers, lab technicians, secretaries and masons.

There have been eight generations of Kirks since they settled in Louisiana. Let each of us thank God for our heritage because without a past, we have no future.

Let us be steadfast, immovable in the word of the Lord. We must, as family, trust and keep God tucked in our hearts, for without Him we would fail, without God, our lives would be rugged, like a ship without a sail.

Let us lean and depend on Jesus. Let Him be your rock, sword, and shield. God is our hope for a strong family and future.

May God forever bless each of you in thought and deed.

July, 1989

The Kirk Family Reunion Chronicle

1983	Detroit, Michigan
1985	Los Angeles, California
1987	Indianapolis, Indiana
1989	Minden, Louisiana
1991	Houston, Texas
1993	Seattle, Washington
1995	Detroit, Michigan

Coming in 1997
Milwaukee, Wisconsin

Postal Order Form

River Vision
P. O. Box 6386
Austin, TX 78762

Ship To:

Name: _____

Address: _____

City: _____ State: _____ Zip: _____

Telephone: (____) _____

Sales tax: Please send 7.25% for books shipped to Texas addresses.

Shipping: Include $3.00 for shipping and handling for first book.
Add $1.00 for each additional book.

Payment: _____ Check   _____ Money Order

Quantity	Item	Unit Price	Total
	It's In The Blood	$9.95	
		Tax	
		Shipping	
		Balance Due	

Postal Order Form

River Vision
P. O. Box 6386
Austin, TX 78762

Ship To:

Name: _____

Address: _____

City: _____ State: _____ Zip: _____

Telephone: (____) _____

Sales tax: Please send 7.25% for books shipped to Texas addresses.

Shipping: Include $3.00 for shipping and handling for first book.
Add $1.00 for each additional book.

Payment: _____ Check _____ Money Order

Quantity	Item	Unit Price	Total
	It's In The Blood	$9.95	
		Tax	
		Shipping	
		Balance Due	